Exclusive distributors:
Music Sales Limited
8/9 Frith Street,
London W1V 5TZ,
England.
Music Sales Pty Limited
120 Rothschild Avenue,
Rosebery, NSW 2018,
Australia.

This book © Copyright 1989 by
Wise Publications
UK ISBN 0.7119.1919.4
Order No AM76274

Arranged by Daniel Scott
Music processed by Barnes Music Engraving

Music Sales complete catalogue lists thousands of
titles and is free from your local music shop, or direct from
Music Sales Limited. Please send £1.75 in stamps for postage to
Music Sales Limited, 8/9 Frith Street, London W1V 5TZ.

Printed in England by
J.B. Offset Printers (Marks Tey) Limited
Marks Tey, Essex

p a s t p r e s e n t

WISE PUBLICATIONS
London/New York/Sydney

THEME FROM HARRY'S GAME

Words & Music by Paul Brennan

STRINGS/VOICES
No rhythm

Mysteriously – slow

CLOSER TO YOUR HEART

Words & Music by Ciaran Brennan

It's out in the o - pen, you might as well be

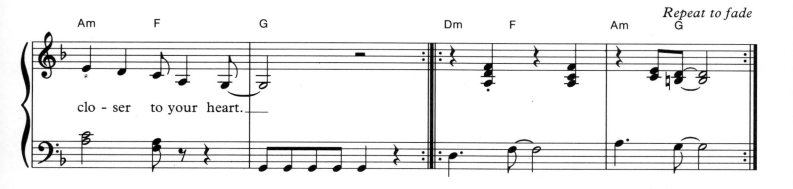

clo - ser to your heart.

2. Tossing and turning and burning dreams across the night
   Forever searching
   Silently waiting for such a long time
   But will I know tomorrow if you will be mine.

3. So it's the same old story when someone just tells you
   That the harder they come yes! The harder they fall
   By taking it easy no matter what people say
   And time will heal all your troubles away.

ALMOST SEEMS (TOO LATE TO TURN)

Words & Music by Paul Brennan

3. Now the anger's gone,
   It leaves behind the pain, again.
   Where did we go wrong?
   Let go my shadow pass by me.

THE HUNTER

Words & Music by Paul Brennan

STRINGS (rh)
Bass guitar (lh)
Rock. 16 Beat
Steady 4

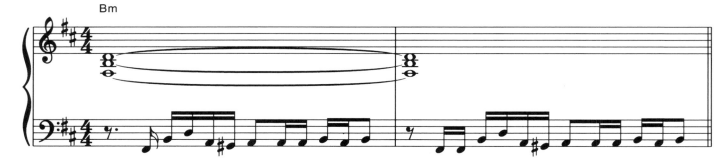

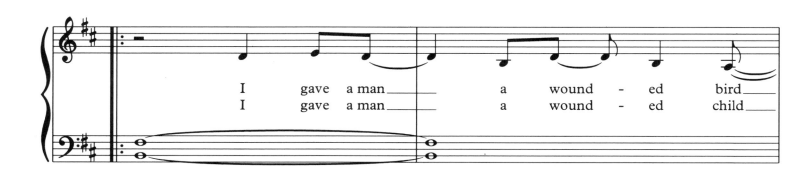

I gave a man _____ a wound - ed bird _____
I gave a man _____ a wound - ed child _____

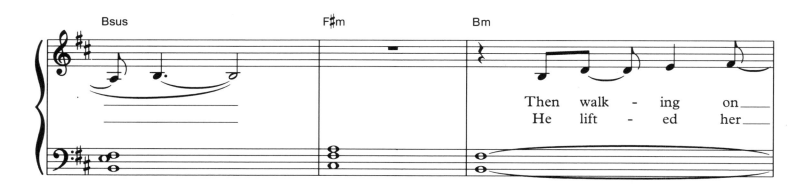

Then walk - ing on
He lift - ed her _____

__ I ov - er - heard _____
__ and then __ she cried _____

He said

all a-long,_____ the hun-ter._____

10

LADY MARIAN

Music by Ciaran Brennan

HARP/STRINGS
No Rhythm

Slow Ballad

SIRIUS

Words & Music by Paul Brennan

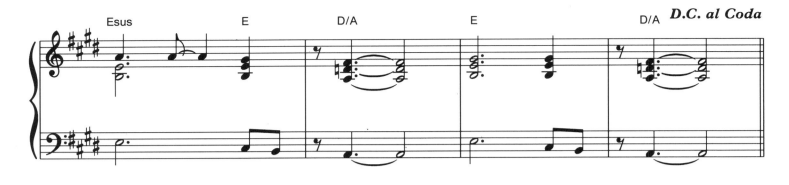

Si - ri - us _____ we'll see who cares Si - ri - us _____ for those that

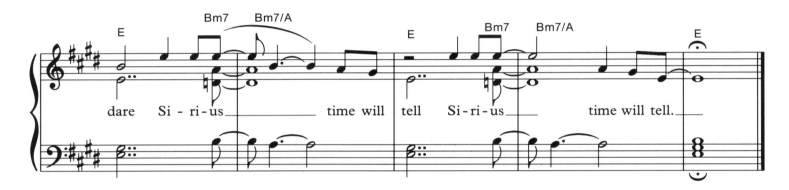

dare Si - ri - us _____ time will tell Si - ri - us _____ time will tell. ____

2. Our ocean's a red sea,
But you won't change your ways.
Move in close as the giants stare on.
The money and the power unite, cast aside.
A guiding star lights the way.

3. The brightness in the sky,
Light years we've tried
As our children's echoes become lonely cries.
The money and the power divide us, cast aside.
A guiding star lights the way.

Sirius, Sirius.
And we'll see who cares
For those that dare,
The time will tell, time will tell.

COINLEACH GLAS AN FHÓMAIR

Traditional Arranged by Clannad

ACOUSTIC GUITAR/PIANO
No Rhythm

sadh nó 'r bord_____ loinge 'triall_____ 'un

siúil

2. Tá buachaillí na háite seo ag athrú 'gus ag
  éirí teann,
 Is lucht na gcocán ard a'deanamh fárais do mo
  chailín donn;
 Dá ngluaiseadh Rí na Spáinne thar sáile 's a
  shloíte cruinn,
 Bhrúfainn feár is fasach 's bheinn ar láimh le mo
  chailín donn.

3. Ceannacht buaibh ar aontaí dá mbínn agus mo
  chailín donn,
 Gluais is tar a cheádsearc nó go dté mind thar
  Ghaoth Bearra 'nonn;
 Go scartar óna chéile barr na gcraobh agus
  an eala ón toinn
 Ní scarfar sinn ó chéile 's níl ach baois
  daoibh a chur in bhur gcionn.

WORLD OF DIFFERENCE

Words & Music by Ciaran Brennan

PIANO/STRINGS/VOICES
No rhythm
Slow 4

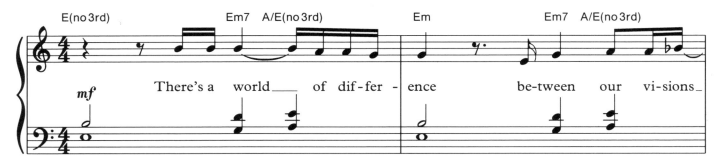

There's a world___ of dif-fer - ence be-tween our vi-sions___

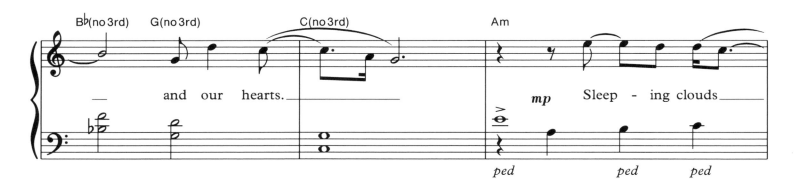

___ and our hearts.___ Sleep - ing clouds___

___ stares the moon___ when do we re-cog-nise_____

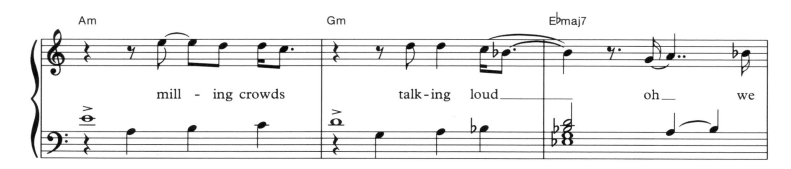

mill - ing crowds talk-ing loud_____ oh___ we

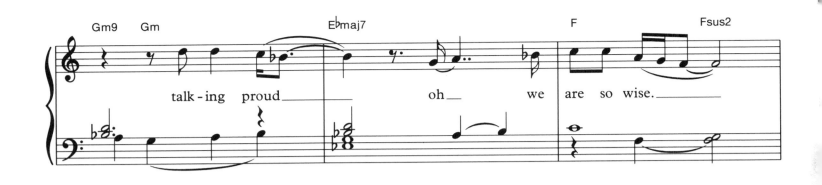

talk-ing proud_____ oh____ we are so wise.____

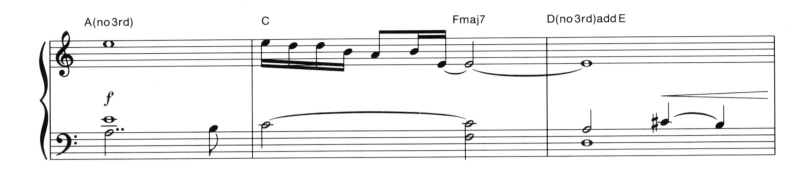

Add rhythm (Slow rock)

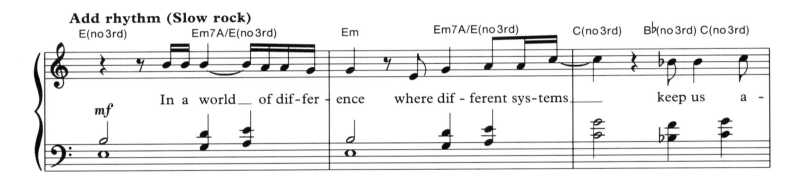

In a world____ of dif-fer - ence where dif - ferent sys-tems____ keep us a -

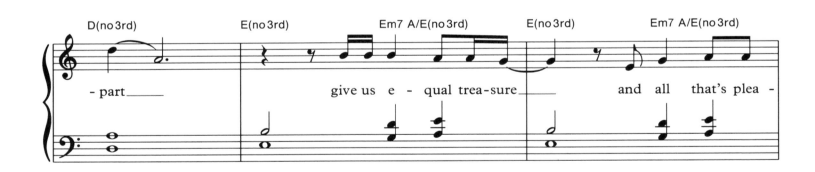

- part_____ give us e - qual trea-sure____ and all that's plea -

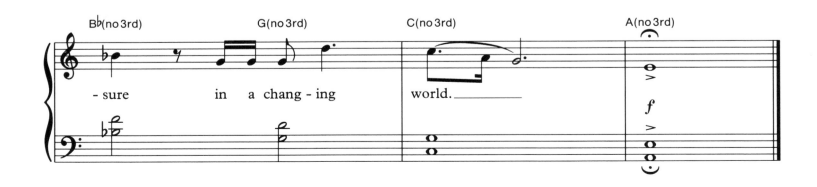

- sure in a chang - ing world._____

IN A LIFETIME

Words & Music by Ciaran Brennan & Paul Brennan

No rhythm
Moderato

Gentle rock

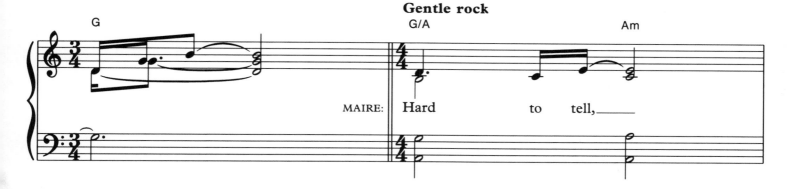

MAIRE: Hard to tell,___

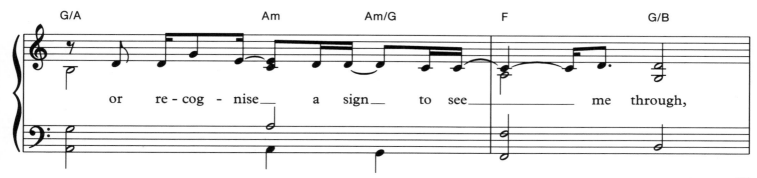

or re-cog-nise___ a sign___ to see___ me through,

-less the sound save your bo-dy's soul, Un-less it dis-ap-pears,

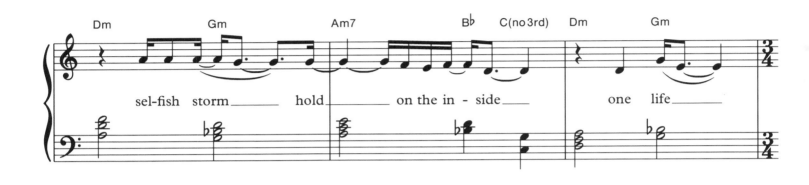

sel-fish storm hold on the in - side one life

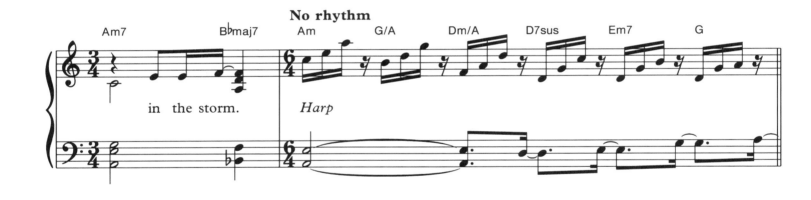

No rhythm

in the storm. *Harp*

Repeat to fade

In a life-time, in a life-time.

ROBIN (THE HOODED MAN)

Words & Music by Ciaran Brennan

BRASS
No Rhythm
Steady beat

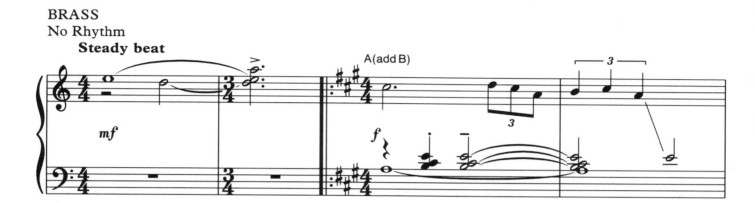

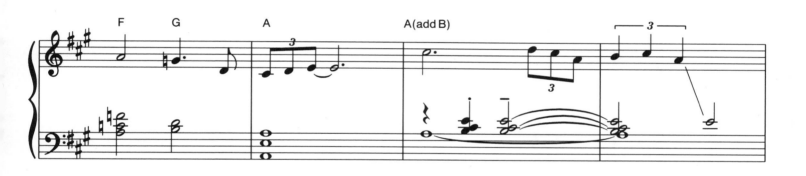

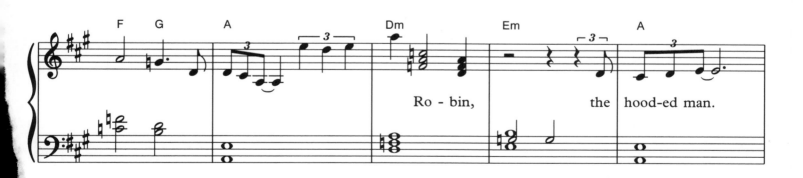

SOMETHING TO BELIEVE IN

Words & Music by Ciaran Brennan

PIANO/ELEC. PIANO
Rock

All the things — they pro - mised, they're al-ways lies. _____ Ah, _____

_____ well it's some - thing. _____ Ah, _____

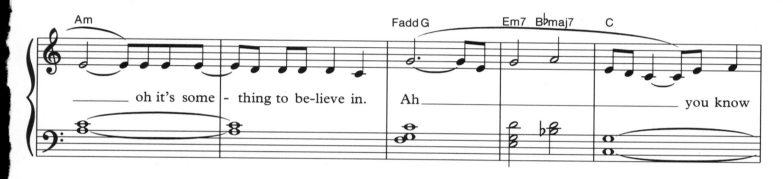

_____ oh it's some - thing to be-lieve in. Ah _____ you know

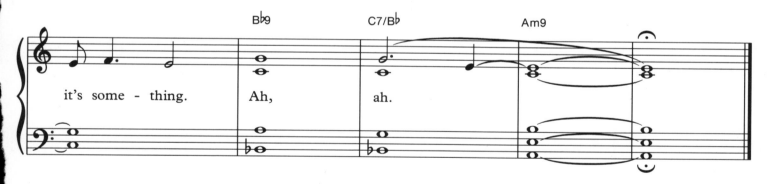

it's some - thing. Ah, ah.

2. Every little once in a while you take a chance to win on a turning card.
   But it may be hard.
   We could be fooled on the merry-go-round, but I'm trying to find
        Something to believe in, to believe in.
   All the things they promised, you know they always lie.
   Ah, ah, ah, ah, it was something
   Ah, ah, ah, something to believe in.
   Ah, ah, ah, something to believe in
   Ah, ah, ah, ah, you know it's something, ah, ah, ah.

3. I've been willing and strong all along, through chilling times
        in a sea of heart-break.
   Where you give and take, I won't give in to promises
   Until I find something to believe in, to believe in.

NEWGRANGE

Words & Music by Ciaran Brennan

GUITAR

Brisk 4 Em

1. There is___ a place___ on the east, mys - te - ri - ous ring, a

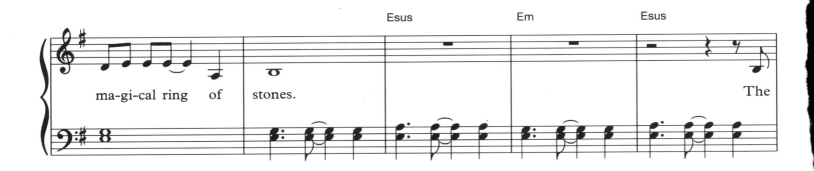

ma-gi-cal ring of stones. The

Dru - ids lived___ here once they said,___ for - got - ten is the race___

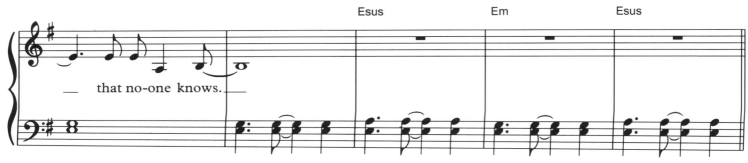

___ that no-one knows.___

Rum de rum rud a deir-im Ó rum de rum rud a deir-im Ó Ó_____

Rum de rum rud a deir-im Ó rum de rum rud a deir-im Ó Ó_____

Fine

Recorder/Strings

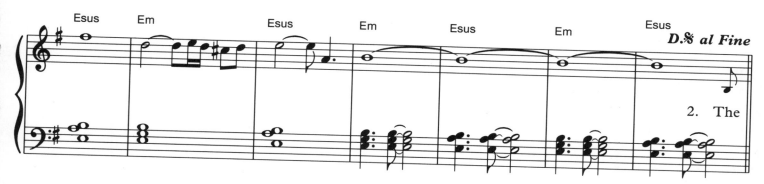

D.S al Fine

2. The

2. The circled tomb of a different age,
    Secret lines carved on ancient stone.
    Heroic kings laid down to rest,
    Forgotten is the race that no—one knows.

3. Wait for the sun on a winter's day,
    And a beam of light shines across the floor.
    Mysterious ring, a magical ring,
    But forgotten is the race that no—one knows.

BUACHAILL AN EIRNE

Traditional Arranged by Clannad

ELEC. PIANO/GUITAR
No rhythm
Simply

Bua - chaill ón ___ Éir - ne mé's bhréag - fainn féin ___

cai - lín ___ deas óg; ___ Ní iarr -

- fainn bó spré ___ lé - ithe ___ tá mé féin ___ saib -

- hir ___ go leor, ___ 'S liom Cor -

2. Buachailleacht bó, mo leo, nár chleacht mise ariamh
   Ach ag imirt 's ag 'ol 's le hógmhná deasa fá shliabh
   Má chaill mé mo stór ní dó' gur chaill mé mo chiall,
   A's ní mó liom do phóg ná 'n bhróg atá 'r caitheamh le bliain.

3. A chuisle 's a stór ná pós an seanduine liath
   Ach pós a' fear óg, mo leo, mur' maire sé ach bliain
   Nó beidh tú go fóill gan ó nó mac os da chionn
   A shilleadh a'n deor tráthnóna nó'r maidin go trom.

WHITE FOOL

Words & Music by Paul Brennan

16 Beat

With rhythm and excitement

Rot - haí an t'saoil ag cás-adh leo____ Níl im-each úaidh go deo.

Da-oine corr an t'saoil ag góid leo__ Níl cu-ma leo go fóill. Rot-haí an t'saoil ag cás-adh leo__ Níl

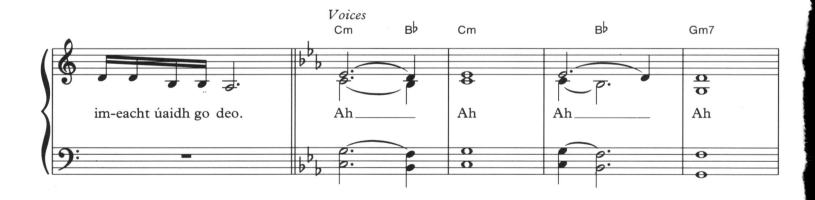

im-eacht úaidh go deo. Ah____ Ah Ah____ Ah

White fool come to a new land. There's a dark moon on the sand. Then

SECOND NATURE

Words & Music by Ciaran Brennan

PIANO/GUITAR
16 beat
Rock

With excitement

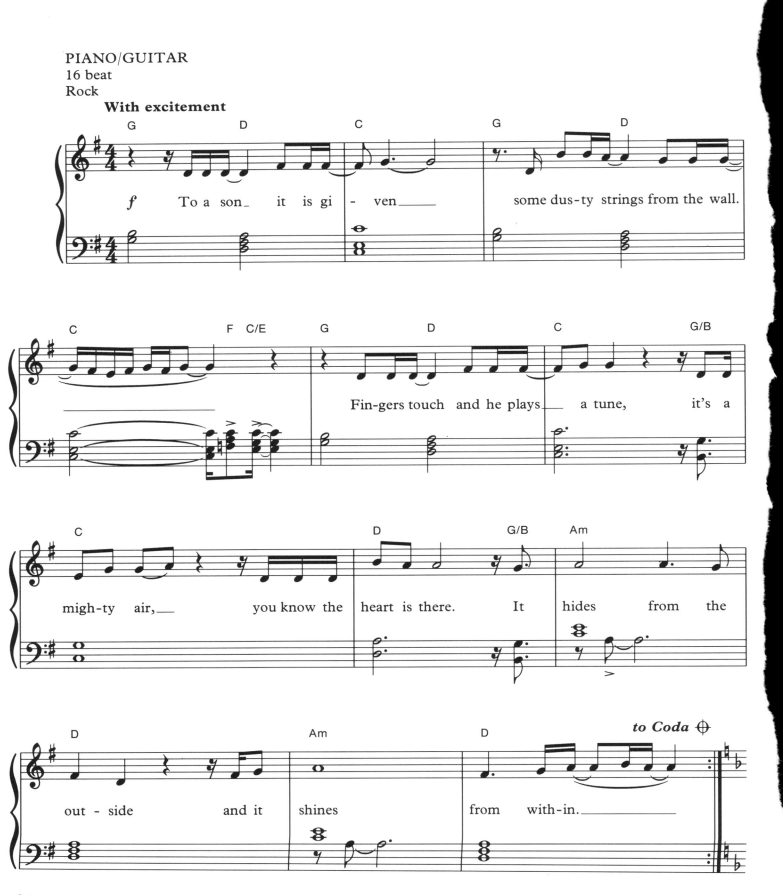

Se-cond na - ture.

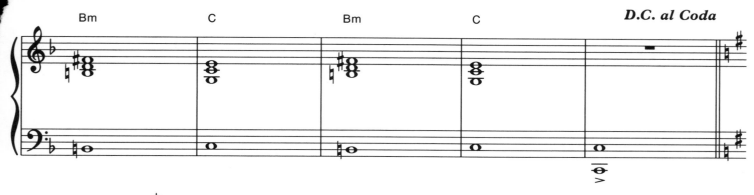

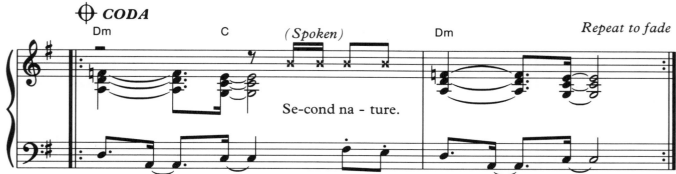

Se-cond na - ture.

2. A ready pen for a picture
   Fine scribes lead the way
   Focus lens direct eyes that see
   The gifted hands
   Through timeless sands

   It hides from the outside
   And it shines from within

3. When nature takes you for a stroll
   Down an avenue with so much soul
   Pleasure, gifts and the ornaments
   The creation found "in the moving cloud"

   It hides from the outside
   And it shines from within
   The kind that keeps holding on

   Second nature, second nature.

10837   11/90